CARING FOR GRAY TREE FROG

A GUIDE TO GRAY TREE FROGS HABITAT, DIET, PRO'S AND CON'S, MANAGEMENT AND KEEPING THEM AS PETS

DR HUNTER DAVIS

Table of Contents

Introduction

With their endearing personality and striking traits, gray tree frogs captivate enthusiasts and make fascinating and unique pets. Scientifically referred to as Hyla versicolor, these frogs are endemic to North America and well-known for their remarkable ability to change color from gray to vivid green in order to blend in with their environment. The purpose of this Introduction is to give a thorough overview of the care and maintenance of gray tree frogs as pets, including their native environment and traits.

Origins and Natural Environment

In North America, gray tree frogs are mostly found in grasslands, marshes, and woodland environments. They are climatically tolerant because of their wide distribution, which includes the southeast of the United

States and certain areas of Canada. It is essential to comprehend their natural habitat in order to recreate an appropriate environment for them in captivity.

Physical attributes

Large, round toe pads that let them climb and cling to surfaces give these small amphibians a unique appearance. Their bodies can vary in size from 1.5 to 2 inches, displaying a small and nimble frame. They have granular skin. Interestingly, they can efficiently disguise thanks to their capacity to change color, which adds a fascinating element to their visual attractiveness.

Way of Life and Conduct

The majority of the time, gray tree frogs are nocturnal animals that are active at night and exhibit colorful habits like climbing, jumping, and vocalizing. Their distinctive trill, which sounds like an insect or bird, gives their appeal aural depth. To create an environment that is suitable to their natural activities, it is essential to understand their behaviors.

Things to Think About Before Owning a Pet

Potential owners need to think about a number of things before deciding to adopt a gray tree frog as a pet. These include being aware of the commitment required, building a suitable enclosure, and being ready for the unique requirements of this species. The health of these fascinating amphibians is greatly enhanced by careful planning and study.

Owners' Responsibilities

There are more duties associated with owning a gray tree frog than just setting up an enclosure. Responsible ownership includes feeding on a regular basis, keeping an eye on health, and preserving the best possible environment. This section will walk potential owners through the necessary steps to guarantee their pet's wellbeing.

Legal Aspects to Take into Account

It's important to be informed of any local or regional laws pertaining to the ownership of amphibians before purchasing a gray tree frog. Certain locations might have limitations or permission needs, which highlights how crucial it is to follow the law in order to encourage responsible pet ownership.

Constructing a Fit Environment

It's critical to create an environment that closely resembles gray tree frogs' natural habitat. This include the following: choosing a suitable enclosure, offering the proper substrate, including climbing chances, and keeping humidity and temperature at ideal levels. In addition to improving the frogs' quality of life, a well-designed environment also increases their general health and lifespan.

dietary needs

For the sake of gray tree frogs, it is essential to comprehend their dietary requirements. We'll get into appropriate food choices, feeding plans, and the value of a varied diet in this part. A food rich in nutrients and well-balanced supports the frogs' general vitality, energy levels, and growth.

Health Tracking and Typical Problems

It's crucial to get regular health examinations to spot any possible problems early. This part will cover how to keep an eye on the frog's physical condition, spot symptoms of disease, and take care of common medical problems. Gray tree frog health and happiness depend heavily on proactive management and timely veterinarian assistance.

Managing and Communicating

Even though they don't usually interact much, it's still necessary for both the owner and the frog to know how to handle them properly. In order to minimize stress and create a secure and comfortable experience, this section will provide advice on when and how to handle these sensitive creatures.

Breeding-Related Issues

This section will examine the requirements and factors for successful breeding of gray tree frogs for those who are interested in trying their hand at breeding them. Through the intriguing process of raising new generations, this information will help fans from designing breeding habitats to comprehending reproductive behaviors.

Possibilities for Education and Recreation

Gray tree frogs present exceptional educational possibilities in addition to the delights of pet ownership. The integration of these amphibians into educational initiatives to promote awareness of amphibian conservation and biodiversity will be covered in this section. It will also touch on recreational aspects, like enjoying the inherent value of these fascinating creatures and witnessing their natural activities.

In summary

The goal of this lengthy introduction is to provide anyone thinking about getting a gray tree frog as a pet a solid basis. Prospective keepers can begin this wonderful path with knowledge and compassion by learning about the origins, physical traits, behaviors, and duties of ownership. This guide paves the way for a rewarding and engaging experience in the realm of gray tree frog friendship, covering everything from creating a suitable environment to taking care of health issues and investigating breeding opportunities.

Chapter 1

Selecting the Right Enclosure

A vital first stage in guaranteeing your gray tree frog's happiness and wellbeing is selecting the ideal enclosure. This in-depth guide will take you step-by-step through the process of choosing the ideal enclosure, covering everything from habitat type and size to the necessary components to furnish your aquatic friend with a cozy and engaging space.

Recognizing Natural Habitat

Understanding the native environment of gray tree frogs is crucial before getting into the finer points of enclosure selection. Usually, these amphibians can be found around woodland places where there are water sources. A variety of trees, shrubs, and leaf litter make up their surroundings, offering them climbing chances as well as cover. You can build a captive environment that nearly matches their natural environments by duplicating these components.

Size and Type of Enclosure

An important factor in the general health of your gray tree frog is the enclosure's size. As a general guideline, one adult frog should have at least 10 gallons of room, plus extra for each extra frog. Given how adept climbers gray tree frogs are, vertical space is essential. They can engage in activities like climbing and hiding that they would naturally do in a taller enclosure with branches and vegetation. For your enclosure, think about going with a glass or acrylic terrarium since they are both quite aesthetically pleasing and easy to maintain. Make sure there is enough ventilation to keep the enclosure's air quality at its best. Although they should be secured to prevent escapes, screen tops are great for ventilation.

Selection of Substances

Selecting the appropriate substrate is crucial in order to replicate the forest floor that gray tree frogs often inhabit. A soft and moisture-retaining basis is created by combining leaf litter with coconut coir or sphagnum moss. This preserves humidity levels inside the container while also promoting the frogs' natural habits.

Scaling Buildings and Hideouts

Being arboreal, gray tree frogs spend a large portion of their time in trees and other elevated areas. Include a variety of climbing structures in the enclosure, including as branches, vines, and cork bark, to accommodate this habit. Not only do these components present chances for physical activity, but they also serve as hiding places, which helps your frogs feel less stressed.

Temperature and Lighting Factors to Take Into Account

Gray tree frog health depends on maintaining the proper temperature. Generally speaking, the optimum temperature range is 68°F to 78°F (20°C to 26°C). To reach this range, use a low-wattage heat source in conjunction with room temperature. A full-spectrum UVB light can also be installed to mimic natural sunlight and encourage the synthesis of vitamin D3, which is necessary for the absorption of calcium.

Controlling Humidity

Maintaining the proper humidity levels is essential for the health of gray tree frogs, as they like a humid habitat. Aim for a 50% to 70% humidity range. This can be accomplished by adding moisture-retaining substrate and often misting the enclosure. Using a hygrometer to check humidity levels guarantees that your frogs' environment stays ideal.

Water-related Features

Gray tree frogs benefit from having a small water dish in their enclosure since they are naturally drawn to water sources. The dish should be sufficiently big to allow the frogs to submerge themselves without being too deep to risk drowning. To keep the water clean and fresh, change it frequently.

Plant Selection

In addition to adding to the enclosure's aesthetic appeal, live plants improve the gray tree frogs' general health. Choose non-toxic plants that do well in damp environments, such pothos, ferns, and bromeliads. By helping to break down garbage, live plants also contribute to the maintenance of air quality.

Enhancement and Invigoration

Intelligent and inquisitive, gray tree frogs gain from both physical and mental stimuli. Include innovative components such as feeding puzzles, climbing obstacles, or rotating hiding areas to add environmental stimulation. This enhances their natural activities and keeps them interested, making their time in captivity more satisfying.

Upkeep and Cleaning

Maintaining a clean and healthy living space for your gray tree frogs requires frequent cleaning. Eliminate excrement, excrement, and shed skin right away. On a regular basis, thoroughly clean the enclosure, replacing the substrate, wiping down the surfaces, and disinfecting the accessories. This regular upkeep is essential to keeping your frogs' environment at its best and preventing the growth of dangerous bacteria.

Observation and Modification

The secret to comprehending your gray tree frogs' particular requirements and preferences is observation. Keep a regular eye on their eating habits, conduct, and general health. When necessary, modify the environmental settings to account for seasonal variations and other circumstances. Additionally, take prompt action to address any indications of illness or stress.

Presenting Several Frogs

Take into account the potential social dynamics and hierarchies that may arise if you intend to house more than one gray tree frog. Make sure that each frog has access to resources, as well as enough space and hiding places. Keep a watchful eye on interactions because there is a chance of hostility or resource competition. A well-thought-out enclosure can reduce the likelihood of confrontations.

Individualization and Tailoring

Although there are fundamental rules for building an appropriate cage, since every frog is different, customisation is essential to satisfying personal tastes. Observe how your gray tree frog engages with different parts of the enclosure and adapt as necessary. With this customization, you can be confident that your pet will flourish in its captivity as well as survive it.

To sum up, choosing the ideal enclosure for your gray tree frog is a complex procedure that necessitates giving considerable thought to its natural habitat, habits, and requirements. Your pet will thrive and be happy if you provide an enclosure that is both the right size and equipped. Every little thing affects your gray tree frog's general health and well-being, which promotes a rewarding and engaging relationship. These little things range from substrate selection to temperature control and environmental enrichment.

Chapter 2

Establishing the Perfect Habitat

Creating the perfect home for your gray tree frog is a challenging but worthwhile endeavor that entails emulating their natural surroundings to guarantee their happiness and well-being. This comprehensive tutorial will take you step-by-step through the process of building a habitat that closely resembles natural settings, including topics like substrate, décor, lighting, temperature, humidity, and more.

Examining Indigenous Environments

It is essential to carry out in-depth research on the natural habitats of gray tree frogs before beginning any habitat development efforts. These frogs are typically found near water sources in forested environments.

Designing an appropriate captive environment requires knowledge of the unique flora, fauna, and environmental conditions of their natural habitat.

Choosing the Correct Enclosure

Selecting the appropriate enclosure is the first step towards constructing the perfect habitat. If you want easy upkeep and clear visibility, go for a glass or acrylic terrarium. To encourage appropriate air circulation, make sure the enclosure has enough ventilation, either through mesh or screen tops. With a minimum of 10 gallons needed for each adult frog, the enclosure's size should be determined by the number of frogs and their anticipated adult size.

Selecting the Proper Substrate

The substrate serves as the habitat's framework, regulating humidity levels and giving your gray tree frog a cozy place to sit. Sphagnum moss and coconut coir combine to provide a soft, moisture-retaining ground that resembles the forest floor. Use leaf litter to mimic the organic matter that is degrading in their natural habitat and to provide a natural touch.

Making Room for Climbing

Because gray tree frogs are expert climbers, it is crucial to provide them with appropriate climbing structures for their physical and mental well. Add branches, vines, and bark made of cork to replicate the vertical features found in their native environment. These buildings offer hiding places, vantage positions for surveying their surroundings, and climbing chances.

Announcing the Hiding Places

For gray tree frogs to feel less stressed and more secure, hiding spots are essential. In order to construct hiding places throughout the enclosure, use a variety of shelters, such as half logs, hollowed-out cork bark, or artificial plants. Because frogs are arboreal by nature, make sure these hiding spots are easily accessible and spaced out over the habitat's levels.

Controlling Temperature

Gray tree frogs depend on the proper temperature being maintained for their wellbeing and activity. One side of the enclosure should have a low-wattage heat source to create a thermal gradient. The frogs are able to select their favorite temperature zone as a result. Maintain the surrounding air temperature between 68°F and 78°F (20°C and 26°C). Maintaining a temperature within the ideal range requires routine thermometer monitoring.

Putting Full-Spectrum Lighting in Place

Exposure to artificial full-spectrum UVB lighting or natural sunshine is beneficial for gray tree frogs. The production of vitamin D3, which is necessary for the absorption of calcium and general health, is aided by UVB lighting. Set up the lighting so that it replicates the day-night cycle of the natural light source. Make sure the frogs have places to hide from the sun when necessary.

Keeping the Ideal Humidity Levels

Gray tree frogs need a humid environment to survive, and keeping their skin and respiratory system at the right humidity levels is essential. A consistent spray of dechlorinated water contributes to the humid atmosphere. Track humidity levels with a hygrometer; a range of 50% to 70% is ideal. Based on the unique requirements of your frogs and the local climate, change the frequency of misting.

Including a Dish for Shallow Water

Gray tree frogs gain by having a small water dish in their habitat because they are naturally associated with water sources. This dish does several tasks, such as offering a place to soak, encouraging hydration, and raising the habitat's general humidity level. To stop the development of bacteria, keep the water clean and replace it frequently.

Choosing Living Plants

Living plants not only enhance the habitat's aesthetic appeal but also improve the gray tree frogs' general health. Select non-toxic plants like orchids, bromeliads, ferns, and pothos. Live plants add natural beauty to the enclosure, provide hiding places, and aid in maintaining humidity. Make sure the plants you've chosen are appropriate for the frogs and the environment of the enclosure.

Enhancement of Environment

Given their intelligence, gray tree frogs gain from both physical and mental stimulation. Introduce innovative features like climbing structures, different textures, and interactive feeding methods to incorporate environmental enrichment. By offering chances for investigation and interaction, these modifications support the frogs' normal habits and improve their quality of life overall.

Frequent Upkeep and Cleaning

For the sake of your gray tree frogs' health and wellbeing, you must keep their habitat clean. Eaten food, excrement, and shed skin should be removed as soon as possible to avoid the growth of dangerous bacteria. Clean the substrate, enclosure surfaces, and décor on a regular basis. Periodically disinfect equipment to maintain a clean living space.

Observation and Modification

To fully comprehend the unique requirements and preferences of your gray tree frogs, observation is essential. Keep a regular eye on their eating habits, conduct, and general health. Take into consideration seasonal variations and other relevant aspects while adjusting environmental settings, and take prompt action to alleviate any indications of illness or stress. This continuous observation guarantees that the environment will continue to support the health of the frogs.

Personalization according to Preferences

Although there are fundamental rules for designing a perfect home, every gray tree frog is different. Observe how your frogs engage with various components of the cage and change the setup as necessary. Individual preference-based customization guarantees your pets' survival and even thrive in their captivity.

Recreational and Educational Components

Include recreational and instructional components in the habitat to keep the frogs and their caregivers interested. Informational items, interactive feeding stations, and observation posts might all fall under this category. You may make your time with your gray tree frogs more enriching by creating an environment that encourages curiosity and learning.

In summary, designing the perfect habitat for gray tree frogs is a deliberate and dynamic process that needs close attention to detail and a thorough comprehension of their requirements and natural behaviors. Everything from choosing the right substrate to controlling the temperature, adding climbing structures, and providing enrichment goes into ensuring the general health of these fascinating frogs. By creating an atmosphere that is similar to their natural habitat, you give your gray tree frogs a safe, fascinating place to live and show off their behaviors, which will make for a rewarding and long-lasting friendship.

Chapter 3

Guidelines for Nutrition and Feeding

For your gray tree frogs to be healthy and happy, feeding and nutrition are essential. This all-inclusive book will offer thorough insights into the food requirements, feeding practices, and nutritional factors that are crucial for guaranteeing the best possible growth, vitality, and lifespan for these fascinating amphibians.

Recognizing the Gray Tree Frogs' Natural Diet

In the wild, gray tree frogs consume a variety of foods, the main ones being tiny insects, spiders, and other invertebrates. It is essential to provide a range of live prey items that meet their nutritional needs in order to mimic their natural diet in captivity. Moths, fruit flies, crickets, and tiny insects are examples of common prey. Providing your gray tree frogs with a varied and balanced diet guarantees that they will get all the nutrients they need for good health.

Selecting Prey Items High in Nutrients

The key to providing gray tree frogs with the food they require is to choose prey that is high in nutrients. By feeding the prey wholesome food before presenting it to the frogs, a technique known as "gut-loading," the prey's nutritional value is increased. Feeder insects such as crickets can be fed commercial gut-loading meals or wholesome fruits and vegetables like carrots and leafy greens.

How Often You Feed

Because they are nocturnal creatures, gray tree frogs often feed in the evening. Giving them food in the evening or at night reflects their nocturnal eating habits. Feeding adult gray tree frogs every two to three days is generally beneficial. Juveniles may need to be fed more frequently—sometimes even every day—in order to support their rapid growth. It's crucial to watch the frogs' activity and modify the feeding plan in accordance with each one of their unique requirements.

Portion sizes and Consumption Monitoring

Provide prey that fits the frog's mouth in terms of size. To avoid any choking hazards, the size of the prey should be proportionate to the size of the frog. During feeding, keep an eye on the frogs to make sure they easily swallow their food. In order to keep the enclosure clean, adjust portion amounts according to each frog's unique metabolism and hunger. You should also take out any uneaten prey items.

Vitamin and Calcium Supplementation

Supplementation is an essential part of nutrition for gray tree frogs, particularly in captivity where it may be difficult to mimic the richness of their natural diet. For the purpose of preventing calcium deficits and ensuring appropriate bone development, it is imperative to dust prey foods with a premium calcium powder that contains vitamin D3. Furthermore, giving them a multivitamin supplement once or twice a month fills in any nutritional gaps that might exist.

Hydration with Diet and Misting Techniques

A large amount of the hydration that gray tree frogs receive comes from their food and the moisture in their surroundings. Providing hydrated prey items helps increase their consumption of water, such as insects that have been gut-loaded with fruits high in water. Regular sprinkling of the enclosure also acts as an extra source of hydration and aids in maintaining humidity levels. Make sure a shallow dish of clean, dechlorinated water is available for the frogs to soak in.

Seeing How People Eat

You may learn a lot about your gray tree frogs' appetite and general health by watching them while they eat. In good health, frogs hunt actively, demonstrating curiosity and dexterity in snagging prey. A sudden drop in appetite or a reluctance to eat are examples of changes in feeding behavior that may point to underlying health problems. Frequent monitoring enables the early identification of possible issues, enabling fast intervention when necessary.

Making the Switch to Captive Diets

It's critical to aid in the adjustment process for gray tree frogs who have recently been acquired or are switching from diets that include wild caught to captive-caught food. It is possible to learn the frogs' preferences by providing a range of prey items and experimenting with different feeding sources. During this period of transition, it is important to have patience so that the frogs can gradually adjust to their new surroundings and food sources.

Preventing Obesity and Overfeeding

While giving someone sufficient and nourishing food is important, overfeeding can result in obesity and related health problems. Although gray tree frogs have enormous appetites, it's important to find a balance between giving them enough food to meet their nutritional demands and not too much. Maintaining a healthy weight, modifying portion amounts, and keeping an eye on physical condition all contribute to your frogs' general wellbeing.

Taking Special Dietary Considerations Into Account

Gray tree frogs may require extra nutritional attention under some circumstances. For instance, certain diets may be necessary for people with certain medical conditions or those recuperating from illnesses. Speaking with a veterinarian who specializes in amphibian care might offer tailored advice on dietary modifications and supplementation to address certain health issues.

Feeding Methods and Promoting Organic Activities

Use methods that promote natural behaviors to improve the eating experience for your gray tree frogs. Make use of feeding ledges, provide interactive feeding equipment, or conceal prey items inside the enclosure. These methods improve the frogs' mental and physical health while igniting their hunting impulses. You may customize the feeding experience to your frogs' unique preferences by experimenting with various feeding techniques.

Keeping an eye on and modifying feeding plans

Like all living things, gray tree frogs can vary over time in terms of their appetite, metabolism, or food choices. Ongoing nutritional support is ensured by routinely reviewing and modifying their feeding programs in light of their unique demands and health status. Revision of portion sizes, investigation of novel prey items, and consultation with veterinarian as necessary are components of a comprehensive and adaptive feeding strategy.

Opportunities for Education Through Eating

Feeding time offers special learning opportunities for viewers and keepers alike. Use this opportunity to pay great attention to the frogs' activities, methods of hunting, and interactions with their prey. This first-hand knowledge helps you better understand your gray tree frogs' innate tendencies and builds a more rewarding and instructive bond with them.

In order to maintain the general health, growth, and vigor of gray tree frogs, feeding and nutrition are essential components of care. You lay the groundwork for their wellbeing by comprehending their natural diet, choosing nutrient-dense prey, establishing a balanced feeding plan, and adding the right supplements. Ensuring a comprehensive approach to their nutritional management involves keeping an eye on feeding behaviors, accommodating personal preferences, and getting veterinarian advice when necessary. By feeding your gray tree frogs with consideration, you help them to thrive and maintain a long-lasting friendship that will provide you and the frogs with a rewarding and enjoyable experience.

Chapter 4

Recognizing the Behavior of Gray Tree Frogs

Comprehending the habits of gray tree frogs is essential to giving them the best care possible and developing a happy bond with these fascinating reptiles. This thorough manual will explore many facets of their behavior, including natural activities, communication, preferred environments, mating habits, and reactions to confinement.

Nature at Night and in Trees

The nocturnal nature of gray tree frogs (Hyla versicolor) means that they are most active at night. These frogs display arboreal behavior in their natural habitat, spending a large amount of time in trees, shrubs, and other raised structures. Their physical features, such as their big toe pads that let them climb and cling to surfaces, are a reflection of their arboreal lifestyle.

They can show these natural behaviors in captivity when their environment is replicated with hiding spots and climbing structures. You may better understand your pet's preferences and build a home that honors their nocturnal habits by keeping an eye on their nighttime activities.

Color-Changing Skills

The capacity of gray tree frogs to change color is one of its most remarkable behavioral characteristics. This adaptive system facilitates thermoregulation in addition to concealment. The mottled gray or brown color of gray tree frogs can change to a vivid green tint in reaction to their surroundings or environmental conditions. By reflecting or absorbing sunlight, their capacity to change hue helps them not only blend in with their surroundings but also control body temperature.

These color shifts, which can be controlled by variables including stress levels, temperature, and light intensity, can be seen in captivity and offer insight into how they perceive their surroundings. They can make use of this innate tendency for camouflage when their habitat is designed to provide a variety of colors and textures.

Speaking and Listening

The vocalizations of gray tree frogs are well-known, especially in the breeding season. Frog males use cries to mark their territories and draw in females. The calls are similar to those of a bird or an insect, but they differ in frequency and pattern. Frogs use vocalizations to define their territory, convey their presence, and indicate that they are ready for mating. These vocalizations are essential to their communication.

Vocalizations made by gray tree frogs in captivity can reveal information about their social dynamics. Keepers may be able to see this unique element of their behavior by creating a setting that resembles their natural breeding conditions, which may trigger these vocalizations. It's important to remember, too, that not all frogs kept in captivity will vocalize, and that their behavior may be influenced by stress or other external circumstances.

Behaviors Specific to a Territory

During the breeding season, when male gray tree frogs compete for advantageous sites to attract mates, territorial behaviors are most noticeable. In the wild, they might mark out areas close to water supplies so they can show off to prospective partners by vocalizing. In captivity, this territorial behavior can also be seen, especially if there are several frogs living in one enclosure. Having plenty of room, hiding places, and climbing frames can all assist reduce the likelihood of confrontations arising from territorial actions.

Instincts for Hunting and Eating

The hunting instincts of gray tree frogs are really good, especially when it comes to taking down live prey. They hunt for tiny insects, spiders, and other invertebrates in the wild. During feeding sessions, their hunting tendencies can be shown in captivity. These frogs use their dexterity and modified tongue to precisely grasp their prey.

Keepers can learn about their innate instincts and assess their appetite, hunting style, and affinity for specific prey items by observing their feeding habits. Using interactive feeding strategies, including hiding prey or using feeding ledges, can improve their innate hunting tendencies.

Disguise & Blending in

A vital component of gray tree frog behavior is hiding and camouflage, which act as defense tactics against potential predators. During the day, these frogs in their natural habitat hide out in plants, leaf litter, or other hidden places. Their capacity to alter hue provides an extra degree of concealment, enabling them to fit in perfectly with their environment.

In order to mimic this behavior in captivity, plenty of hiding places must be provided, such as plants, hollowed-out cork bark, or other shelter-producing structures. They can provide important details about their comfort level and stress reactions by keeping an eye on their color changes and hiding spot preferences.

Reproductive and Breeding Behaviors

Gray tree frogs exhibit particular reproductive habits during breeding season. In order to aid the laying of eggs, male frogs will vocalize in order to attract females. If this wooing is successful, the male will then grip the female in an amplexus. Usually, eggs are laid in wet places like leaf litter or in shallow water. After hatching, the tadpoles go through metamorphosis and become young frogs.

Replicating breeding-friendly environments in captivity, such as offering a water source and suitable environmental cues, may encourage reproductive behaviors. However, some factors are frequently necessary for effective breeding, and not all captive settings may be able to maintain the full reproductive cycle.

Reactions to Changes in the Environment and Captivity

When their environment changes or they are kept in captivity, gray tree frogs may react in different ways. In particular, stress might show up as behaviors like decreased activity, changing coloration, altered hunger, or excessive hiding. For gray tree frogs kept in captivity, reducing stresses, offering a well-planned habitat, and allowing for acclimatization throughout changes all contribute to a more cozy and happy experience.

Frogs can exhibit distinct habits and preferences on an individual basis. While some people could be more shy and like to hide in quiet places, others might be more gregarious and eager to explore their surroundings. Respecting and acknowledging each frog's uniqueness encourages a more individualized approach to their care.

Opportunities for Enrichment and Observation

Observing gray tree frogs on a regular basis yields a lot of information about their preferences and general well-being. Keepers can customize care procedures for individual frogs by observing how they interact with their surroundings, react to changes, and interact with one another (if there are numerous frogs).

Gray tree frogs kept in captivity have an even higher quality of life when environmental enrichment is included. Interactive features that promote exploration and elicit natural behaviors include climbing frames, creative hiding places, and a variety of materials. By experimenting with various enrichment choices, keepers can discover their preferences and establish an interesting and dynamic environment.

Cues from the Environment for Seasonal Behaviors

Gray tree frogs may react to environmental stimuli by displaying seasonal habits. In the wild, hibernation and breeding are triggered by variations in temperature and photoperiod. Even while the seasonal changes of the wild may not always be replicated in captivity, behavior can be affected by changing some elements, like illumination and temperature. For instance, giving gray tree frogs a small temperature decrease throughout the winter could simulate a state akin to hibernation.

Managing and Considering Interactions

Because they are often delicate when handled, gray tree frogs can become stressed out by repeated or incorrect handling. Because of the permeability of their thin skin, they can absorb things from human hands. If handling is required, it is important to handle with clean, moist hands and with gentle touch. Reduce the amount of handling to minimize stress and always let frogs move at their own speed.

The greatest way to interact with gray tree frogs is to observe them. Keepers can learn to respect their natural instincts and reactions by calmly studying their habits. Although frogs kept in captivity may eventually grow acclimated to their caregivers, interaction with them should be handled gently and considerate of their comfort zones.

Monitoring of Behavior and Health

Assessing the health and well-being of gray tree frogs requires careful observation of their activity. A person's behavior, including changes in food, posture, or level of tiredness, might be a good indicator of potential health problems. Frequent observation guarantees a proactive approach to their care, together with regular health exams and environment modifications.

In summary

One exciting and satisfying part of raising these fascinating amphibians is getting to know the habits of gray tree frogs. Their vocalizations, territorial actions, nocturnal and arboreal lifestyle, and reactions to confinement are just a few of the behaviors that reveal important information about their preferences and general well-being. Gray tree frogs can thrive in a nurturing environment that is helpful and rewarding if caretakers observe, respect, and accommodate their natural impulses. Harmonious relationships are facilitated by deliberate care techniques and regular interaction, which enables keepers to recognize and value the distinctive personalities and habits of these amazing amphibians.

Chapter 5

Medical Care and Typical Problems

Maintaining the health and welfare of gray tree frogs is an essential duty for those who care for them. This extensive manual will address many facets of healthcare, typical medical conditions, prophylactic actions, and suitable reactions to preserve the best possible physical and mental state for these fascinating frogs.

Recognizing Normal Physiology and Behavior

It's important to have a foundational grasp of typical gray tree frog physiology and behavior before diving into health treatment. Keepers can identify any abnormalities that could indicate possible health issues by routinely observing the behaviors of their animals, including their vocalizations, eating habits, and interactions with their surroundings. The traits of gray tree frogs include their ability to change color, their nocturnal habits, and their arboreal lifestyle. Recognizing whether anything may be off is made easier with an understanding of these normal actions. Furthermore, getting acquainted with their typical physiological characteristics—such as body condition, posture, and skin texture—provides a foundation for evaluating health.

Establishing the Ideal Environment for Health

Gray tree frog health is fundamentally dependent on a well-designed habitat. You enhance their general well-being by imitating their natural habitat. The right substrate, climbing structures, hiding spots, and ambient factors like humidity, temperature, and lighting are all important components. Sustaining ideal settings promotes the frogs' capacity to engage in their natural behaviors and helps avoid stress-related problems. Keeping the enclosure clean on a regular basis, offering a range of enrichment activities, and providing a balanced meal are all essential to fostering a healthy environment.

Typical Health Problems and Symptoms

Even with careful maintenance, gray tree frogs might have health problems. Early intervention depends on identifying common health issues and comprehending their signs. Among the many common health problems are:

Skin Issues:

- Symptoms include irregular skin tone, sores, ulcers, and changes in skin texture.

- Potential causes include exposure to irritants, unhygienic enclosures, and poor environmental conditions.

- Intervention: Keep the habitat in top condition, deal with any possible environmental stressors, and seek the advice of a veterinarian for the best course of action.

infected respiratory systems:

- Symptoms include wheezing, open-mouth breathing, labored breathing, and increased mucus production.

- Possible causes include irritating exposure, insufficient humidity, and bacterial or fungal infections.

- Intervention: Seek veterinarian care for respiratory illnesses, maintain hygiene, make sure there is enough ventilation, and adjust humidity levels.

Parasitic Diseases:

- Weight loss, fatigue, irregular stools, or parasites that are visible are symptoms.
- Potential causes include contaminated prey, filthy surroundings, or parasite exposure.
- Intervention: Place afflicted frogs in quarantine, administer suitable antiparasitic drugs under veterinary supervision, and put preventive measures in place.

MBD, or metabolic bone disease:

- Symptoms include weakness, deformity, fatigue, or trouble moving.

- Potential causes include inadequate nutrition, inadequate UVB exposure, and insufficient calcium and vitamin D3 intake.
- Intervention: Make sure UVB lighting is available, feed a well-balanced food with the right supplements, and seek supportive treatment from a veterinarian.

Issues Connected to Stress:

- Reduced activity, appetite loss, color changes, or excessive hiding are some of the symptoms.
- Potential causes include improper handling, unsuitable surroundings, or environmental modifications.
- Intervention: Reduce sources of stress, offer safe havens, and make sure the surroundings are stable and appropriate.

Accidents:

- Signs include obvious wounds, limping, or unusual posture.

- Potential causes include mistreatment, environmental dangers, and aggressive encounters between frogs.

- Intervention: In case of severe injuries, seek veterinary assistance, provide a safe environment, and isolate frogs that are hurt.

Preventive Health Actions

It's crucial to prevent health problems as well as treat them when they do occur. By taking preventive action, common health problems are less likely to occur and the general health of gray tree frogs is maintained. Important health precautions include:

Appropriate Diet

- Provide a broad and well-balanced diet of suitably sized live prey.

- Before feeding, stuff prey items' stomachs with wholesome nutrients.

- Apply a calcium supplement including vitamin D3 to prey items.

Keeping the Ideal Habitat Conditions:

- Keep the enclosure clean on a regular basis to stop the growth of bacteria and fungi.

- Provide hiding spots, climbing structures, and an appropriate substrate.

- Make sure the humidity and temperature are appropriate.

Keeping an eye on environmental parameters

- To keep an eye on the temperature and humidity, use a trustworthy thermometer and hygrometer.

- Use UVB lighting to assist in the synthesis of vitamin D3.

- When applicable, emulate seasonal variations in nature.

Health examinations and quarantines:

- Before adding additional frogs to an established group, place them in quarantine.

- Check your weight, behavior, and skin condition on a frequent basis.

Reducing Stress:

- Reduce handling, particularly when things are unpleasant.

- To lessen stress, provide a stable and safe setting.

- Steer clear of abrupt changes in routine or environment.

Observation and Documentation:

- Observe frog interactions and behavior on a regular basis.
- Note weight, feeding regimens, and any changes you see.
- Keep an eye out for any changes in skin tone, texture, or alignment.

Veterinary Medical Attention:

- Form a rapport with a veterinarian who specializes in the care of frogs.
- Immediately seek veterinarian assistance if you see any symptoms of sickness.
- Observe any suggested immunization schedules.

Practices for Quarantine

One concern associated with reintroducing new frogs into an established group is the introduction of possible infections. Quarantine procedures are used to stop the spread of contagious diseases. Before reintroducing the young frogs to the main habitat, they can be observed for any symptoms of disease by being isolated in a separate cage for a certain amount of time.

The newly arrived frogs are kept in a clean, distinct enclosure as part of quarantine procedures. Keep an eye on their general health, eating patterns, and demeanor at this time. Prior to integrating them into the established group, appropriate veterinary care can be sought if any signs of disease or parasite illnesses appear.

Continual Health Examinations

Regular health examinations are a proactive way to keep an eye on gray tree frogs' wellbeing. Individual frogs should have routine evaluations performed on them, which should include skin examinations, weight checks, and feeding habit observations. By keeping track of any behavioral or physical changes, keepers can see possible problems before they become serious.

Looking for Veterinary Medical Attention

Gray tree frog health depends on developing a relationship with a veterinarian skilled in amphibian care. Regular examinations, diagnostic exams, and frog-specific treatment regimens are all possible components of veterinary care. Seeing a veterinarian as soon as possible if any irregularities or symptoms of sickness are noticed improves the chances of successful interventions.

Considerations for Captive Breeding

In addition, keepers who are interested in captive breeding must take health concerns into account. Careful consideration must be given to tadpole care, breeding environment, and reproductive habits. Successful captive breeding depends on maintaining ideal environmental conditions, providing good breeding habitats, and supplying a food high in nutrients.

The wellbeing of adult frogs and their progeny should be guaranteed by ethical breeding methods used in captivity. Breeding practices that sustain genetic diversity and species conservation are beneficial.

Maintaining Records and Documentation

Maintaining thorough records is an important way to keep an eye on gray tree frog health and welfare. Keeping records could involve:

Feeding Timetable:

- Note the kinds and quantities of prey that are available.
- Keep track of any adjustments in feeding habits or appetite.

Environmental Factors:

- Note the humidity and temperature.
- Keep track of any alterations made to the habitat.

Behavioral Insights:

- Record the interactions and behaviors you see.
- Take note of any variations in activity levels, posture, or colors.

Health Examinations:

- Note the weight measurements.

- Note any anomalies or symptoms of disease.

Veterinary Appointments:

- Maintain a log of your veterinary visits.
- Make a note of any prescription drugs or therapies.

Maintaining records makes it easier to spot trends, monitor changes over time, and supply crucial data for veterinarian consultations. Gray tree frogs benefit from proactive health treatment made possible by this systematic approach, which also enhances their general wellbeing.

Gray tree frog health requires a multifaceted approach that includes habitat design, proactive measures, regular health assessments, and timely intervention when necessary. Keepers may create a setting that supports the physical and emotional well-being of these fascinating amphibians by learning about their typical activities, identifying common health issues, and taking proactive health measures. A comprehensive health care plan includes practicing ethical breeding, maintaining thorough records, and building a relationship with an experienced veterinarian. Gray tree frogs can flourish in captivity with committed care and attention to their particular needs, giving their keepers the satisfaction of a lasting and meaningful companionship.

Chapter 6

Managing and Communication Pointers

Gray tree frogs need to be handled and interacted with with care and consideration. Because of their delicate skin, these fascinating amphibians need a safe and stress-free environment to flourish at their best. This thorough guide will go over handling methods, interaction issues, and strategies for building a happy bond with gray tree frogs.

Knowing the Anatomy and Physiology of Frogs

Understanding the anatomy and physiology of gray tree frogs is essential before attempting to handle them. These frogs have sensitive, porous skin that is capable of absorbing things from human hands, such as chemicals and oils. Excessive handling can interfere with gas exchange, which is facilitated by their skin, an important respiratory organ. Additionally, adhesive toe pads in gray tree frogs allow them to climb and adhere to a variety of surfaces. These toe pads are delicate and easily broken if not handled properly. Injuries might also result from stress-related activities like trying to flee or jumping excessively.

When Not to Touch Something:

- When Under Stress: Steer clear of handling when under stress, such as following a move or significant environmental changes.

- Breeding Season: Handling frogs should be avoided during this time of year as they may become more territorial or agitated.

- After Feeding: Handling right after following a meal may result in stomach problems or regurgitation.

- When Shedding: Handling frogs should be avoided during the shedding process as they may become more sensitive.

Appropriate Management Methods:

Use these correct methods while working with gray tree frogs to reduce stress and potential injury:

- Wet Your Hands:

Before handling, wet your hands with fresh, dechlorinated water. This lessens the chance of chemicals from your skin getting on the frog's fragile skin.

- **Manage Calmly and Gently:**

Be cool when approaching and gently handle the frog. Steer clear of clutching or abrupt motions since these can exacerbate tension.

- **Assist the Body:**

With both hands, support the frog's body so that it rests on your palms. Steer clear of squeezing or exerting too much pressure.

- **Steer clear of jumping distances:**

Treat the frog on a cushiony, safe place to avoid bruises from jumping. Due to their agility, frogs can leap suddenly.

- **Time Limit for Handling:**

Shorten handling sessions to reduce tension. Prolonged manipulation may cause pain.

- See How Frogs Act:

Observe how the frog behaves while being handled. Put it back in its enclosure if it exhibits indications of stress, such as color changes, vocalizations, or efforts to flee.

- Steer clear of frequent handling:

Reduce the frequency of handling to lessen tension. Long-term or frequent handling can cause health problems.

Tips for Interaction:

Although handling should be kept to a minimum, there are still methods to engage with gray tree frogs that support their natural behaviors:

- Note:

Take time to study the frogs in their natural environment. This enables you to enjoy their innate habits and interactions with their surroundings.

- Feeding Relationship:

Make use of interactive feeding strategies, such hiding prey or employing feeding ledges. Their innate hunting instincts are heightened by this.

- Activities for Enrichment:

Add components that will enhance the surroundings, including interactive features, different textures, or climbing structures. These extras encourage investigation and cerebral stimulation.

- Teaching Resources:

Place instructional resources or observation spots all around the enclosure. This promotes curiosity and permits passive interaction.

- Videography and photography:

Capture moments with a camera or a video. This enables you to record their actions without having to engage in direct physical contact.

- Changes in the Environment:

Make small adjustments to the surroundings, such as moving climbing structures or creating new hiding places. This offers something fresh and inspires investigation.

- Group Behavior:

Examine the dynamics of the frogs' group if you are maintaining more than one. Observing frogs interact with one another can be fascinating and provide details about their social tendencies.

Establishing a Secure and Invigorating Space:

Make sure the frog's habitat is well-designed and meets their natural needs in order to promote pleasant interactions. Take into account the following elements:

- Sufficient Room:

Give the enclosure enough room to accommodate climbing, exploring, and natural movement.

- Climbing Frameworks:

Incorporate branches, climbing frames, and hides to mimic their arboreal characteristics. This offers chances to explore and engage in physical activities.

- Protected Hideouts:

Provide safe havens for frogs to withdraw to when they sense a threat to their safety. Stress is reduced as a result.

- Range of Textures:

To create an intriguing atmosphere, use a range of substrate textures, such as sphagnum moss or coconut coir.

- Living Plants:

Include living plants that provide hiding places and enhance the enclosure's attractiveness.

- Interactive Kitchen Sinks:

Establish feeding stations that promote instinctive hunting techniques. This may entail using feeding ledges or concealing prey items.

- Points of Observation:

Establish observation vantage points for the frogs and yourself. This makes passive engagement possible and improves the experience as a whole.

Honoring Personal Preferences:

Since every gray tree frog is different, so are their comfort zones and tastes. While some people could be more gregarious and able to put up with some handling, others might want little to no interaction. Respecting their uniqueness makes the atmosphere happier and less stressful. Observe each frog's reaction to handling and other interactions. If a certain frog exhibits signs of tension or discomfort on a regular basis, minimize handling and concentrate on more comfortable ways to connect with them.

Youngsters and Frog Communication:

It's important to watch over kids carefully and teach them safe handling methods when they engage with gray tree frogs. Youngsters should be careful, refrain from making abrupt movements, and comprehend that reducing stress is crucial for the frogs' welfare. Children should be taught about the natural activities of gray tree frogs and encouraged to take ownership of their maintenance. The educational experience can be improved by limited, gentle handling under adult supervision and supervised observation.

Managing During Medical Examinations:

Routine handling should be kept to a minimum, however there are times when veterinary exams or health checks call for handling. When managing due to health concerns:

- Be Kind and Effective:

Treat the frog with efficiency and gentleness. Cut down on handling time to lessen tension.

- Make Use of Wet Gloves:

If possible, keep your hands or gloves moist to avoid coming into direct contact with the frog's skin.

- Promptly return to the enclosure:

Return the frog to its enclosure as soon as possible after the health examination. Establish a safe and comfortable workplace.

- Cut Down on Handling Frequency:

Carefully plan your health examinations to reduce the amount of times you are handled for medical purposes.

Taking Care of Things for Breeding:

The following rules should be followed while handling for breeding purposes, such as to aid in amplexus or egg-laying:

- Examine Typical Behaviors:

Let the natural actions come to pass. Keep an uninhibited eye on courting, amplexus, and egg-laying.

- Establish Appropriate Breeding Conditions:

Make sure the enclosure has all the necessary elements for breeding, such as a water source and hiding places.

- Reduce Disturbances:

Reduce interference as much as possible to support normal reproductive processes during the breeding season.

- Observing Tadpoles:

If the breeding process is successful, keep an eye on the tadpoles individually to make sure they're healthy and receiving the right care for their growth.

Handling Acts of Aggression:

When several gray tree frogs are kept in one enclosure, watch how they interact to look for indications of hostility. Territorial disputes, vocalizations, and physical confrontations are examples of aggressive behaviors. If hostility is seen:

- Give Enough Room:

Make sure there is adequate room inside the enclosure to reduce territorial disputes.

- Establish Dedicated Areas:

To build distinct areas inside the enclosure, add more hiding places and structures.

- Keep an eye on group dynamics:

Observe the dynamics of the group carefully. Consider putting the frogs into separate enclosures if the antagonism doesn't go away.

- If A Quarantine Is Required:

If hostility results in stress or damage, the afflicted frog should be temporarily isolated for observation or quarantine.

Handling Behaviors Associated with Stress:
Stress-related behaviors can take many different forms, like changes in color, hiding more often, or less activity.

If actions associated with stress are noticed:

- Assess the surrounding environment:

To guarantee the ideal humidity, temperature, and general comfort, evaluate the habitat's parameters and make any necessary modifications.

- Reduce the amount of handling:

Minimize handling to ease tension. Provide steady surroundings and safe hiding places.

- Observe Modifications in Conduct:

Keep an eye on behavioral changes and take quick action to alleviate any possible stressors.

- Speak with a Veterinarian:

See a vet with experience caring for frogs if stress-related symptoms continue or get worse.

In summary

Gray tree frogs need to be handled and interacted with with care and consideration. Both keepers and frogs benefit from an understanding of their anatomy, respect for individual preferences, and use of appropriate handling techniques. Alternative means of connection, such feeding, observation, and habitat enrichment, enable keepers to cultivate a rewarding and engaging relationship with these fascinating amphibians, even though direct handling should be limited. Gray tree frogs are beautiful and amazing creatures, and keepers can appreciate their beauty and wonder while contributing to their lifespan in captivity by providing a secure and stimulating environment that is tailored to each frog's specific needs.

Chapter 7

Breeding-Related Issues

For devoted frog lovers, breeding gray tree frogs can be a fulfilling and instructive endeavor. This thorough tutorial will go over many areas of breeding considerations, such as setting up a habitat, mating habits, laying eggs, taking care of tadpoles, and rearing froglets. The success and welfare of these fascinating amphibians are enhanced by knowing the nuances of breeding gray tree frogs, regardless of your level of experience.

Knowing the Species of Gray Tree Frogs:

There are various species of gray tree frogs, such as the Cope's gray tree frog (Hyla chrysoscelis) and the Eastern gray tree frog (Hyla versicolor). Even though they are similar in that they may change color and are arboreal, it is crucial to recognize the particular species in order to make the right breeding decisions. Make sure you understand the particular needs and behaviors related to the species you are caring for.

Sexual Maturity and Age:

Depending on their diet and surroundings, gray tree frogs usually attain sexual maturity between the ages of one and two. It is important to wait until frogs are sexually mature before attempting to breed them. During the breeding season, males acquire darker throats called vocal sacs, which they utilize to attract mates. Males are often smaller than females.

Making a Breeding Environment:

A crucial element in the successful reproduction of gray tree frogs is the establishment of an appropriate breeding environment. When establishing a breeding environment, take into account the following elements:

- Sufficient Size of Enclosure:

Make sure the habitat is roomy enough to support the behaviors of mating and producing eggs. Territorial disputes are less likely in a larger enclosure.

- Climbing Frameworks:

Incorporate plants, branches, and climbing structures to resemble their natural arboreal habitat. These buildings could be places for mating and hiding.

- Source of Water:

To help with egg laying, provide a shallow water source (a dish filled with dechlorinated water is a good example). Make sure the water is fresh and replaced frequently.

- Temperature and Humidity:

Keep the temperature and humidity levels adequate. Replicating these differences can encourage breeding in gray tree frogs, which may display reproductive behaviors in response to seasonal variations.

- Lighting at Night:

In order to replicate the natural cycle, use lighting at night. Due to their nocturnal lifestyle, gray tree frogs depend on nighttime darkness for both their health and mating habits.

- Substance:

Select a moisture-retaining substrate, like sphagnum moss or coconut coir. As a result, the habitat is favorable for tadpole development and egg laying.

- Hideout Locations:

Incorporate safe havens, like vegetation or hollowed cork bark, to provide frogs with a feeling of security throughout the breeding season.

- Living Plants:

Include real plants, which not only improve the appearance but also offer more surfaces for tadpole hiding places and egg attachment.

Behavior and Vocalizations in Breeding:

The vocalizations of gray tree frogs are well-known, especially in the breeding season. In order to establish territories and draw in females, male frogs make calls. The calls are similar to those of a bird or an insect, but they differ in frequency and pattern. Learn the characteristic cries of your species of gray tree frog, as these are essential to their mating rituals.

Among the mating behaviors are:

- Amplexus:

The mating embrace, or amplexus, occurs when the male grabs the female to help with egg laying. This behavior can happen in or close to the water source, and vocalizations are frequently a part of it.

- Laying Eggs:

Usually, aquatic habitats with vegetation hanging over water or shallow water are where females lay their eggs. Ascertain whether there are appropriate locations inside the enclosure for the laying of eggs.

- Geographical Exhibitions:

Male frogs have the ability to display their territory by calling and physical contact with other males. Minimizing territorial disputes can be achieved by providing enough space and hiding places.

- Customs of Courtship:

In order to attract and communicate with possible mates, courtship rituals comprise a variety of behaviors, including vocalizations, visual displays, and physical interactions.

Breeders must watch and comprehend these characteristics in order to determine whether their frogs are ready for breeding. Amplexus and egg-laying activities indicate that a breeding episode has been successful.

Care for Tadpoles and Laying Eggs:

The female gray tree frog will deposit eggs after mating, usually in an aquatic setting. Make sure there are places in the cage where the eggs can be laid, like submerged or floating plants. Frequently, eggs are adhered to these surfaces.

Take into account these pointers for caring for tadpoles and depositing eggs:

- Watching Over Egg Clutches:

Keep a close eye on egg clutches to make sure they're safe. Steer clear of disruptions that could cause damage or dislodging.

- Dividing Eggs If Required:

When keeping many frogs in one enclosure, keep an eye out for any possible disruptions. To avoid injury, think about separating egg clutches or individual frogs if hostility or interference is noticed.

- Development of Tadpoles:

Tadpoles of the gray tree frog go through metamorphosis and become juvenile frogs. Provide the right environment for tadpole development, which includes the right temperature, water quality, and hiding places.

- Tadpole nourishment:

Provide a variety of food sources for tadpoles, including as algae, finely crushed plant material, and commercial tadpole food. Healthy development is supported by adequate nutrition.

- Sorting Out Tadpoles:

In order to avoid resource rivalry, if there are several tadpoles, you might want to consider putting them in separate containers. This makes it possible to track their growth more carefully.

- Slow Transition from Air to Land:

Give tadpoles the chance to gradually move to land as they grow. Incorporate areas where froglets that are just forming can emerge from the water and reach the land.

Bringing Up Froglets:

It is important to pay attention to the unique requirements of froglets as they change from aquatic tadpoles to terrestrial juveniles in order to raise them successfully. Think about the following elements:

- Land Features:

Introduce land characteristics to help froglets move from their watery habitat, including mossy surfaces or climbing frames.

- Transitional Diet:

Change the diet gradually from tadpole food to suitably sized live prey. Present tiny creatures such tiny waxworms, fruit flies, or pinhead crickets.

- Preserving Ideal Conditions:

Make sure the froglets are growing in the ideal humidity and temperature ranges. Keep an eye on their actions and modify the surroundings as necessary.

- Providing Places to Hide:

Incorporate hiding places into the cage to give froglets protection when they are most vulnerable.

- Monitoring and Health Examinations:

Keep a regular eye on the froglets' health and behavior. Perform health examinations to quickly spot any indications of stress or sickness.

- Changing to an Adult Diet:

Froglets should be gradually introduced to an adult diet of properly sized insects as they mature. Keep an eye on their eating reactions and modify the diet as necessary.

- Keeping Things Clean:

To avoid fungus or germs, keep the cage clean. Remove food scraps and rubbish on a regular basis.

Responsible Breeding and Ethical Issues:

Ethical concerns are part of responsible breeding procedures to guarantee the health of adult frogs as well as their progeny. Think about the following moral issues:

- How Not to Inbreed:

When breeding related individuals, keep in mind that there may be genetic problems. Achieve genetic diversity by purchasing frogs from various suppliers.

- Observing Conservation Guidelines:

Requirements and rules for conservation must be followed while breeding threatened or endangered species. The conservation of amphibian species is aided by ethical breeding.

- Giving Sufficient Care:

Make sure that the frogs' welfare is given first priority during the breeding process. The breeding population's health is influenced by responsible actions, appropriate settings, and enough care.

- How Not to Over Breed:

Take into account your facilities' and resources' capacity before starting any breeding operations. Steer clear of overbreeding, as this may make it difficult to give your children the right care.

- Locating Adequate Residences for Froglets:

Make arrangements for the froglets' placement in appropriate homes. Conscientious breeders take into account the long-term welfare and upbringing of their progeny.

- Teaching Aspiring Owners:

Give prospective frog owners advice and instructional resources. Encouraging knowledgeable and conscientious ownership is part of responsible breeding.

Maintaining Breeding Data Records:

Gray tree frog health and successful reproduction depend on keeping thorough records. Keeping records could involve:

- When to Breed:

Note the dates of the egg-laying, amplexus, and mating events.

- Development of Eggs:

Keep an eye on the growth of the egg clutches and record any anomalies or modifications.

- Growth of Tadpoles:

Observe the tadpoles' growth and development, as well as any behaviors that are noticed.

- Froglet Changeover:

Keep track of the tadpoles' progress into froglets, noting any difficulties or developmental checkpoints.

- Medical Records:

For tadpoles, froglets, and adult frogs, maintain medical records. Keep track of any disease symptoms or veterinarian treatments.

- Details about Genetics:

Preserve genetic data, if applicable, to trace genealogy and prevent inbreeding.

- Data on feeding and the environment:

Keep track of feeding times, dietary compositions, and any ambient condition modifications.

In summary:

The complex process of breeding gray tree frogs includes setting up the habitat, observing mating habits, laying eggs, tending to the tadpoles, and rearing the froglets. Breeders can help preserve these interesting amphibians by knowing their reproductive habits, building a setting that resembles their natural habitat, and giving them the right care at every stage of growth. Comprehensive record-keeping, ethical considerations, and responsible breeding procedures all add to the wellbeing of adult frogs and their progeny. Breeders can enjoy the delight of seeing gray tree frogs in captivity via effort, education, and a passion for amphibian care.

Chapter 8

Interesting Trivia and Facts

There are a lot of interesting facts and trivia about gray tree frogs, which makes them fascinating animals. An extensive look into the fascinating world of gray tree frogs can be had with this collection of interesting facts and trivia, which includes information on their unusual activities and amazing adaptations.

1. Superb Color-Changing Skills:

Gray tree frogs are well known for their remarkable capacity to change color. They can change the color of their skin to blend in with their surroundings; depending on lighting and other environmental factors, it can go from gray to green. They can effectively avoid predators thanks to their ability to blend in with their arboreal environments.

2. The Lifestyle of the Arboreal

Gray tree frogs are mostly arboreal, which means they live most of their lives in trees, true to their name. They are expert tree-dwellers thanks to their unique toe pads with adhesive disks that enable them to climb and cling to a variety of surfaces. This adaptation helps them evade ground-based predators and navigate their vertical homes.

3. Nighttime Pilots:

The nocturnal nature of gray tree frogs is evidenced by their increased activity levels at night. In keeping with their arboreal origins, they lead nocturnal lives that enable them to forage for food, investigate their surroundings, and carry out reproductive processes in the shadow of the night. They can evade diurnal predators thanks to this behavior.

4. Differentiated Voices:

The distinctive vocalizations made by male gray tree frogs are well-known, especially in the breeding season. Their calls are a succession of brief, melodic thrills that sound like insects or birds. Researchers and fans can distinguish between different species of gray tree frogs by listening to their unique calls.

5. Encrypted Species Recognition:

Because of their similar outward looks, distinct species of gray tree frogs can be difficult to distinguish. Cope's gray tree frog (Hyla chrysoscelis) and the Eastern gray tree frog (Hyla versicolor) are two cryptic species with similar morphology. Accurate species identification frequently requires genetic analysis, highlighting the significance of molecular technologies in herpetological study.

6. Freeze-Tolerance During the Cold Season:

The extraordinary adaptation of gray tree frogs allows them to withstand the harsh winter weather. They go into a condition of torpor throughout the winter and can withstand below-freezing temperatures. They accomplish this by letting some of their bodily fluids freeze, which lowers their metabolic rate and stores energy until the weather gets warmer again.

7. Territorial Actions:

Male gray tree frogs engage in territorial activities to create and protect ideal mating places during the breeding season. These tactics include making loud noises to draw attention from women and using calls and physical contact to intimidate potential suitors. Territorial conflicts are frequent, and gaining and protecting a desirable breeding site is frequently necessary for successful mating.

8. Special Toe Protectors for Climbing:

The adhesive disks on the toe pads of gray tree frogs allow them to stick to a variety of surfaces with remarkable traction. Their arboreal existence depends on these toe pads, which enable them to climb trees, maneuver around branches, and even cling to smooth surfaces like glass or leaves.

9. Dietary Insectivorous:

Being insectivores, gray tree frogs mostly feed on a range of tiny invertebrates. Insects include crickets, moths, ants, beetles, and spiders are among their food sources. In their natural environments, their swift reflexes and nimble tongues help them catch prey, making them effective hunters.

10. Unusual Defense Against Predators:
Gray tree frogs have an unusual defense strategy against predators called the "rain call." When they sense a threat, particularly in dry conditions, they make a succession of cries that resemble raindrops. Predators may become confused by this activity, giving the frog a chance to sneak away unseen.

11. Increased Range as a result of Human Activity:
Urbanization and other human activities have unintentionally increased the range of gray tree frogs. Because they are able to adapt to a variety of

conditions, these amphibians have become more common in suburban and even urban settings. Their vast range is facilitated by their capacity to utilize a variety of habitats.

12. Adaptable Breeding Locations:

Gray tree frogs are adaptable when it comes to selecting their mating grounds. It is common for them to lay their eggs in ditches, ponds, and rain-filled containers, but they can also use tree cavities, vegetation hanging over water, or even man-made structures. Their ability to adapt helps them reproduce successfully in a variety of settings.

13. Lifespan in Retention:

If given the best care possible, gray tree frogs can live lengthy lives in captivity. They can survive for more than ten years with good husbandry, which includes an appropriate habitat, a balanced diet, and veterinary care when necessary. Numerous factors, including genetics, environment, and general health, affect longevity.

14. Inflation of the Vocal Sac While Calling:

To generate their characteristic calls, male gray tree frogs use a special mechanism. They inflate their vocal sacs, which are flexible membranes beneath their throats, as they vocalize. The sound produced is amplified by this sac inflation, which improves the cries' ability to draw in possible mates.

15. Adaptations of Amphibians:

Both terrestrial and aquatic adaptations are present in gray tree frogs. They live most of their life in trees, but for breeding and tadpole development, they also need aquatic habitats. Their dual way of life demonstrates their adaptability to living in both aquatic and terrestrial environments.

16. From Tadpole to Frog Transformation:

Gray tree frogs go through an amazing transformation from tadpole to froglet and finally to adult. Significant physiological and morphological changes occur in tadpoles, including the appearance of lungs for air breathing, the growth of hind limbs, and the absorption of the tail. The end result of this process is the development of fully developed froglets.

17. Enchanting Customs of Courtship:

Gray tree frogs have fascinating and complex courtship behaviors. To entice and interact with possible mates, males use activities like vocalizations, displays, and physical contact. Amplexus is the final stage of courtship, during which the male grasps the female to help lay eggs.

18. Strategies for Attaching Eggs:

Gray tree frog females use a variety of techniques to adhere their eggs to appropriate surfaces. Eggs are frequently affixed to floating debris, submerged plants, or vegetation that hangs over water. The eggs' ability to stick to one another securely shields them from potential predators in the aquatic environment.

19. Concerns Regarding Conservation:

Although there isn't currently a worldwide hazard to gray tree frogs, habitat loss, pollution, and the development of infectious illnesses could pose local threats to some populations. The main goals of conservation efforts are to protect their natural habitats, keep an eye on population trends, and comprehend how possible climate change may affect their range.

20. Effect on Control of Insect Pests:

It is advantageous for gray tree frogs to regulate insect populations. They eat insects, which includes beetles, moths, and mosquitoes, among other pests. They emphasize the ecological significance of these pests by aiding in the natural control of pests in their respective environments through their consumption.

21. Favorability in the Pet Industry:

Gray tree frogs have a compelling appearance and reasonably low maintenance needs, which makes them attractive pets. On the other hand, responsible ownership is essential, and potential keepers should confirm that they are able to offer these amphibians suitable habitats, food, and medical attention. Avoiding wild-caught specimens and following conservation rules are two ethical considerations.

22. A Unique Eye Stripe:

A dark eye stripe that runs from the eye down the side of the body is one of the characteristics that set gray tree frogs apart. Their eye stripe and their mottled skin pattern help them blend in better with their arboreal surroundings, providing good hiding from predators and prey.

23. Taking Note of Anuran Anatomy

Researchers and hobbyists can get up close and personal with anuran (frog and toad) anatomy by studying the anatomy of gray tree frogs. A greater understanding of amphibian biology and adaptations can be gained by studying gray tree frogs, which have specific toe pads, vocal sacs, and distinctive skin textures.

24. Individual Variations in Voice:

Individual males in a population of gray tree frogs may differ in their vocalizations' pitch, frequency, and pattern. Within the breeding chorus, these variances might function as a means of individual recognition and communication. These vocal subtleties are used by researchers to analyze population dynamics and differentiate between individuals.

25. Symbolism in Legends:

A variety of cultures and folktales attribute symbolic meaning to frogs, particularly gray tree frogs. They are frequently linked to concepts of metamorphosis, rebirth, and flexibility. Given their affinity for water and amphibious environments, frogs are revered in many cultures as rain and fertility symbols.

In summary:

A plethora of fascinating knowledge and facts can be discovered by investigating the world of gray tree frogs. These amphibians never cease to amaze scientists, enthusiasts, and nature lovers with their amazing color-changing skills, unique vocalizations, and adaptions. Knowing the subtleties of gray tree frogs helps us appreciate their important role in ecosystems and their amazing life path from tadpole to adult tree-dwelling frog, which makes us stewards of their well-being.

Chapter 9

This pet's FAQs and responses

Q1: How long does a gray tree frog live in captivity?

A1: Gray tree frogs can survive in captivity for more than ten years with the right care. Their lifetime is influenced by various factors, including genetics, habitat quality, and general health.

Q2: What is the diet of gray tree frogs?

A2: As insectivores, gray tree frogs consume tiny invertebrates such as crickets, moths, ants, beetles, and spiders. They need a diverse diet to be healthy.

Q3: Are gray tree frogs capable of color change?

A3: It's true that gray tree frogs are well known for their capacity to change color. They can change from gray to green, blending in with their environment to provide a disguise.

Q4: What is the best way to put up a gray tree frog's enclosure?

A4: Construct a large, arboreal setting with climbing features, a water supply, appropriate humidity, and a substrate such as sphagnum moss or coconut coir. Use living plants and hiding places to replicate their natural environment.

Q5: Do novice frog keepers find gray tree frogs to be a suitable choice?

A5: They need special attention even if they are quite manageable. To guarantee optimal well-being, beginners should investigate their demands, particularly with relation to temperature, humidity, and diet.

Q6: How can I determine whether my gray tree frog is ill?

A6: Skin color changes, fatigue, atypical posture, changes in appetite, and weight loss are some of the symptoms of disease. For the purpose of identifying and resolving health difficulties, routine health examinations, behavior observation, and veterinary consultation are essential.

Q7: Is it possible to house several gray tree frogs together?

A7: You can often keep more than one gray tree frog, but keep an eye out for hostility. Give people plenty of room, cover places, and distance them from one another in case territorial disputes occur.

Q8: Are gray tree frogs suitable as kid pets?

A8: Although children may find them intriguing to watch, supervision is necessary to guarantee gentle handling.

Reduce stress, teach kids how to take care of frogs, and put their welfare first.

Q9: How can I encourage my gray tree frogs to breed?
A9: Use variations in humidity and temperature to replicate seasonal shifts. During the breeding season, provide climbing structures, a water source for laying eggs, and keep an eye out for vocalizations and wooing behaviors.

Q10: If my gray tree frog isn't eating, what should I do?
A10: There are a number of things that can cause decreased appetite, such as stress, unfavorable environmental circumstances, or medical disorders. See a vet, go over husbandry procedures, and think about providing a range of prey items to encourage feeding.

Q11: Can I release a gray tree frog that was raised in captivity back into the wild?

A11: Releasing frogs raised in captivity into the outdoors may displace natural populations or bring diseases. Speak with the appropriate local authorities and think about morally righteous options, like finding them appropriate homes.

Q12: What is a safe way to handle a gray tree frog?
A12: To avoid damaging your skin, moisten your hands before handling. To reduce stress, handle softly, provide support for the body, and shorten sessions. If you notice any indications of distress, quickly put the frog back in its enclosure."

www.ingramcontent.com/pod-product-compliance
Lightning Source LLC
Chambersburg PA
CBHW070806260726
48660CB00005B/1734